BFI FILM CLASSICS

Cinema is a fragile medium. Many of the great classic films of the past now exist, if at all, in damaged or incomplete prints. Concerned about the deterioration in the physical state of our film heritage, the National Film Archive, a Division of the British Film Institute, has compiled a list of 360 key films in the history of the cinema. The long-term goal of the Archive is to build a collection of perfect showprints of these films, which will then be screened regularly at the Museum of the Moving Image in London in a year-round repertory.

BFI Publishing has now commissioned a series of books to stand alongside these titles. Authors, including film critics and scholars, film-makers, novelists, historians and those distinguished in the arts, have been invited to write on a film of their choice, drawn from the Archive's list. Each volume will present the author's own insights into the chosen film, together with a brief production history and a detailed filmography, notes and bibliography. The numerous illustrations have been specially made from the Archive's own prints.

With new titles published each year, the BFI Film Classics series will rapidly grow into an authoritative and highly readable guide to the great films of world cinema.

BFI FILM CLASSICS

THE WIZARD OF OZ

....

Salman Rushdie

BFI PUBLISHING

791.4372 WIZ
97833

First published in 1992 by the
BRITISH FILM INSTITUTE
21 Stephen Street, London W1P 1PL

Reprinted 1993

British Library Cataloguing in Publication Data

Rushdie, Salman, *1947–*
The wizard of Oz.
I. Title
791.43090915

ISBN 085170 300 3

Designed by
Andrew Barron & Collis Clements Associates

Typesetting by
Fakenham Photosetting Limited, Norfolk

Printed in Great Britain by
The Trinity Press, Worcester

CONTENTS

. . . .

I

II

For
Angela Carter

A very good wizard
and a very dear friend

Giant hollyhocks

I
....
A SHORT TEXT ABOUT MAGIC

I wrote my first story in Bombay at the age of ten; its title was *Over the Rainbow*. It amounted to a dozen or so pages, dutifully typed up by my father's secretary on flimsy paper, and eventually it was lost somewhere on my family's own mazy journeyings between India, England and Pakistan. Shortly before his death in 1987 my father claimed to have found a copy mouldering in an old file, but in spite of my pleadings he never produced it, and nobody else ever laid eyes on the thing. I've often wondered about this incident. Maybe he never really found the story, in which case he had succumbed to the lure of fantasy, and this was the last of the many fairytales he told me; or else he did find it, and hugged it to himself as a talisman and a reminder of simpler times, thinking of it as his treasure, not mine – his pot of nostalgic, parental gold.

I don't remember much about the story. It was about a ten-year-old Bombay boy who one day happens upon a rainbow's beginning, a place as elusive as any pot-of-gold end-zone, and as rich in promises. The rainbow is broad, as wide as the sidewalk, and constructed like a grand staircase. The boy, naturally, begins to climb. I have forgotten almost everything about his adventures, except for an encounter with a talking pianola whose personality is an improbable hybrid of Judy Garland, Elvis Presley and the 'playback singers' of the Hindi movies, many of which made *The Wizard of Oz* look like kitchen-sink realism. My bad memory – what my mother would call a 'forgettery' – is probably just as well. I remember what matters. I remember that *The Wizard of Oz* (the film, not the book, which I didn't read as a child) was my very first literary influence. More than that: I remember that when the possibility of going to school in England was mentioned, it felt as exciting as any voyage beyond rainbows. It may be hard to believe, but England felt as wonderful a prospect as Oz.

The Wizard, however, was right there in Bombay. My father, Anis Ahmed Rushdie, was a magical parent of young children, but he was also prone to explosions, thunderous rages, bolts of emotional lightning, puffs of dragon-smoke, and other menaces of the type also practised by Oz, the great and terrible, the first Wizard Deluxe. And when the curtain fell away and his growing offspring discovered, like Dorothy, the truth about adult humbug, it was easy to think, as she did, that our Wizard must be a very bad man indeed. It took me half a lifetime to discover that the Great Oz's *apologia pro vita sua* fitted my father equally well – that he, too, was a good man, but a very bad Wizard.

I have begun with these personal reminiscences because *The Wizard of Oz* is a film whose driving force is the inadequacy of adults, even of good adults, and how the weakness of grown-ups forces children to take control of their own destinies, and so, ironically, grow up themselves. The journey from Kansas to Oz is a rite of passage from a world in which Dorothy's parent-substitutes, Auntie Em and Uncle Henry, are powerless to help her save her dog Toto from the marauding Miss Gulch, into a world where the people are her own size, and in which she is never, ever treated as a child, but as a heroine. She gains this status by accident, it's true, having played no part in her house's decision to squash the Wicked Witch of the East; but by her adventure's end she has certainly grown to fill those shoes, or, rather, those ruby slippers. 'Who'd have thought a girl like you could destroy my beautiful wickedness,' laments the Wicked Witch of the West as she melts – an adult becoming smaller than, and giving way to, a child. As the Wicked Witch of the West *grows down*, so Dorothy is seen to have grown up. This, in my view, is a much more satisfactory reason for her new-found power over the ruby slippers than the sentimental reasons offered by the ineffably soppy Good Witch Glinda, and then by Dorothy herself, in a cloying ending that I find untrue to the film's anarchic spirit. (More about this later.)

The weakness of Auntie Em and Uncle Henry in the face of Miss Gulch's desire to annihilate Toto the dog leads Dorothy to think, childishly, of running away from home – of escape. And that's why, when the tornado hits, she isn't with the others in the storm shelter, and as a result is whirled away to an escape beyond her wildest dreams. Later, however, when confronted by the weakness of the Wizard of Oz, she doesn't run away, but goes into battle, first against the Witch, and then against the Wizard himself. The Wizard's ineffectuality is one of the film's many symmetries, rhyming with the feebleness of Dorothy's folks; but Dorothy's difference of reaction is the point.

The ten-year-old who watched *The Wizard of Oz* at Bombay's Metro cinema knew very little about foreign parts and even less about growing up. He did, however, know a great deal more about the cinema of the fantastic than any Western child of the same age. In the West, the film was an oddball, an attempt to make a sort of live-action version of a Disney cartoon feature in spite of the industry's received wisdom that fantasy movies usually flopped. There seems little doubt that the excitement engendered by *Snow White and the Seven Dwarfs* accounts for MGM's decision to give the full, all-stops-out treatment to a 39-year-old book. This was not, however, the first screen version. I haven't seen the silent film of 1925, but its reputation is poor. It did, however, feature Oliver Hardy as the Tin Man.

The movie never really made money until it became a television standard years after its original theatre release, though it should be said in mitigation that coming out a few days before the start of World War II can't have helped its chances. In India, however, it fitted into what was then, and remains today, one of the mainstreams of 'Bollywood' film production.

It's easy to satirize the Hindi movies. In James Ivory's film *Bombay Talkie*, a journalist (the late, touching Jennifer Kendal) visits a studio sound-stage and watches an amazing dance number featuring scantily-clad nautch girls prancing on the keys of a giant typewriter. The director explains that the typewriter is actually 'The Typewriter of Life', and 'We are all dancing out our stories' upon that great machine. 'It's very, um, symbolic,' she suggests. The director, simpering rather, replies: 'Thank you.'

Typewriters of Life, sex-goddesses in wet saris (the Indian equivalent of wet T-shirts), gods descending from the heavens to meddle in human affairs, supermen, magic potions, superheroes, demonic villains and so on have always been the staple diet of the Indian filmgoer. Blonde Glinda arriving at Munchkinland in her magic bubble might cause Dorothy to comment on the high speed and oddity of local transport operating in Oz, but to an Indian audience she was arriving exactly as a god should arrive: *ex machina*, out of her own machine. The Wicked Witch of the West's orange smoke-puffs were equally appropriate to her superbad status.

It is plain, however, that in spite of all the similarities there were important differences between the Bombay cinema and a film like *The Wizard of Oz*. Good fairies and bad witches might superficially resemble the deities and demons of the Hindu pantheon, but in reality one of the most striking aspects of the world-view of *The Wizard of Oz* is its joyful and almost complete secularism. Religion is mentioned only once in the film. Auntie Em, spluttering with anger at gruesome Miss Gulch, tells her that she's waited years to tell her what she thinks of her, 'and now, because I'm a good Christian woman, I can't do so.' Apart from this moment in which Christian charity prevents some good old-fashioned plain-speaking, the film is breezily godless. There's not a trace of religion in Oz itself; bad witches are feared, good ones liked, but none are sanctified; and while the Wizard of Oz is thought to be something very close to all-powerful, nobody thinks to worship him. This absence of higher values greatly increases the film's charm, and is an important aspect of its success in creating a world in which nothing is deemed more important than the loves, cares and needs of human beings (and, of course, tin beings, straw beings, lions and dogs).

The nautch girls in *Bombay Talkie*

The other major difference is harder to define, because it is finally a matter of quality. Most Hindi movies were then and are now what can only be called trashy. The pleasure to be had from such films (and some of them are extremely enjoyable) is something like the fun of eating junk food. The classic Bombay talkie uses scripts of appalling corniness, looks by turn tawdry and vulgar and often both at once, and relies on the mass appeal of its stars and its musical numbers to provide a little zing. *The Wizard of Oz* has stars and musical numbers, but it is also very definitely a Good Film. It takes the fantasy of Bombay and adds high production values and something more; something not often found in any cinema. Call it imaginative truth. Call it (reach for your revolvers now) art.

If *The Wizard of Oz* is a work of art – and, I suppose, its presence in this series indicates that I'm not alone in thinking it is – it's extremely difficult to say who the artist was. The birth of Oz itself has already passed into legend: the author, L. Frank Baum, named his magic world after the letters O–Z on the bottom drawer of his filing cabinet.

Baum had an odd, roller-coaster life. Born rich, he inherited a string of little theatres from his father, and lost them all through mismanagement. He wrote one successful play and numerous flops. The Oz books made him one of the leading children's writers of the day, but all his other fantasy novels bombed. *The Wonderful Wizard of Oz*, and a musical adaptation of it for the stage, restored Baum's finances; but a financially disastrous attempt to tour America promoting his books with a 'fairylogue' of slides and films led him to file for bankruptcy in 1911. After that, living on his wife's money at 'Ozcot' in Hollywood, he raised chickens and won prizes at flower shows. After the small success of an Oz musical, *The Tik-Tok Man of Oz*, improved his finances, he ruined them again by setting up his own movie company, the Oz Film Company, and trying unsuccessfully to film and distribute the Oz books. After two bedridden years, and still, we are told, optimistic, he died in May 1919. His frock-coat, however, lived on into a strange immortality (see page 45).

The Wonderful Wizard of Oz, published in 1900, contains many of the ingredients of the magic potion – all the major characters and events are here, and the most important locations, the Yellow Brick Road, the Deadly Poppy Field, the Emerald City. But the filming of *The Wizard of*

Oz is one of the rare instances of a film improving on a good book. The changes include the expansion of the Kansas section, which in the novel takes up precisely two pages at the beginning before the tornado arrives, and just nine lines at the end; a certain simplification of the storyline in the Oz section – all subplots were jettisoned, such as the visits to the Fighting Trees, the Dainty China Country and the Quadlings that come, in the novel, just after the dramatic high point of the Witch's destruction and fritter away the book's narrative drive; and two even more important alterations. Frank Baum's Emerald City was only green because everyone in it had to wear emerald-tinted glasses; whereas in the movie it really is a futuristic chlorophyll green, except, that is, for the Horse of a Different Colour You've Heard Tell Of. The Horse of a Different Colour changes colour in each successive shot, a change brought about by covering it in a variety of shades of powdered Jell-O. (For this and many other anecdotes of the film's production, I'm indebted to Aljean Harmetz's definitive *The Making of The Wizard of Oz*, published by Pavilion Books in 1989.)

Last and most important of all are the ruby slippers. Frank Baum did not make up the ruby slippers: he called them Silver Shoes. Noel Langley, the first of the film's three credited writers, originally went along with Baum's idea. But in his fourth script, the script of 14 May 1938, known as the DO NOT MAKE CHANGES script, the clunky, metallic and non-mythic silver footwear has been jettisoned, and the immortal jewel-shoes are introduced for the first time, as Harmetz tells us, in shot 114: 'The ruby shoes appear on Dorothy's feet, glittering and sparkling in the sun.'

Other writers contributed important details to the finished screenplay. Florence Ryerson and Edgar Allan Woolf were probably responsible for 'There's no place like home', which, as I'll be arguing, is the least convincing idea in the film (it's one thing for Dorothy to want to get home, quite another that she can only do so by eulogizing the ideal state which Kansas so obviously is not). But there's some dispute about this, too; a studio memo implies that it could have been the associate producer Arthur Freed who first came up with the cutesy slogan. And, after much quarrelling between Langley and Ryerson-Woolf, it was the film's lyricist Yip Harburg who pulled together the final script, and added the crucial scene in which the Wizard, unable to

give the companions what they demand, hands out emblems instead, and to our 'satiric and cynical' satisfaction they do the job. The name of the rose turns out to be the rose, after all.

Who, then, is the *auteur* of *The Wizard of Oz*? No single writer can claim that honour, not even the author of the original book. Mervyn LeRoy and Arthur Freed, the producers, both have their champions. At least four directors worked on the picture, most notably Victor Fleming, who left before shooting ended, however, so that he could make *Gone With the Wind*, ironically enough the movie that dominated the Oscars while *The Wizard of Oz* won just three: Best Song ('Over the Rainbow'), Best Musical Score and a Special Award for Judy Garland. The truth is that this great movie, in which the quarrels, sackings and near-bungles of all concerned produced what seems like pure, effortless and somehow inevitable felicity, is as near as dammit to that will-o'-the-wisp of modern critical theory: the authorless text.

The Kansas described by L. Frank Baum is a depressing place, in which everything is grey as far as the eye can see – the prairie is grey and so is the house in which Dorothy lives. As for Auntie Em and Uncle Henry: 'The sun and wind ... had taken the sparkle from her eyes and left them a sober grey; they had taken the red from her cheeks and lips, and they were grey also. She was thin and gaunt, and never smiled now.' Whereas: 'Uncle Henry never laughed. He was grey also, from his long beard to his rough boots.' The sky? It was 'even greyer than usual'. Toto, fortunately, was spared greyness. He 'saved Dorothy from growing as grey as her other surroundings'. He was not exactly colourful, though his eyes did twinkle and his hair was silky. Toto was black.

It is out of this greyness – the gathering, cumulative greyness of that bleak world – that calamity comes. The tornado is the greyness gathered together and whirled about and unleashed, so to speak, against itself. And to all this the film is astonishingly faithful, shooting the Kansas scenes in what we call black and white but what is in reality a multiplicity of shades of grey, and darkening its images until the whirlwind sucks them up and rips them into pieces.

There is, however, one other way of understanding the tornado.

Dorothy has a surname: Gale. And in many ways Dorothy is the gale blowing through this little corner of nowhere, demanding justice for her little dog while the adults give in meekly to the powerful Miss Gulch; Dorothy who is prepared to break the grey inevitability of her life by running away, and who is so tender-hearted that she then runs back again when told by Professor Marvel that Auntie Em will be sad that she has fled. Dorothy is the life-force of Kansas, just as Miss Gulch is the force of death; and perhaps it is Dorothy's feelings, or the cyclone of feelings unleashed between Dorothy and Miss Gulch, that are made actual in the great dark snake of cloud that wriggles across the prairie, eating the world.

The Kansas of the film is a little less unremittingly bleak than the Kansas of the book, if only because of the introduction of the three farmhands and of Professor Marvel, four characters who will find their 'rhymes', their counterparts, in the Three Companions of Oz and the Wizard himself. Then again, it is also more terrifying, because it adds a presence of real evil: the angular Miss Gulch, with a profile that could carve a joint, riding stiffly on her bicycle with a hat on her head like a plum pudding, or a bomb, and claiming the protection of the Law for her crusade against Toto. Thanks to Miss Gulch, the movie's Kansas is informed not only by the sadness of dirt-poverty, but also by the badness of would-be dog-murderers.

And *this* is the home that 'there's no place like'? *This* is the lost Eden that we are asked to prefer (as Dorothy does) to Oz?

I remember, or I imagine I remember, that when I first saw this film, at a time when I had a pretty good home, Dorothy's place struck me as a dump. Of course, if *I'd* been whisked off to Oz, I reasoned, I'd naturally want to get home again, but then I had plenty to come home for. But Dorothy? Maybe we should invite her over to stay; anywhere looks better than *that*.

I thought one other thought, which I had better confess now, as it gave me a sneaking regard for the Wicked Witch, and, some might say, a secret sympathy for all persons of her witchy disposition which has remained with me ever since.

I couldn't stand Toto. I still can't. As Gollum said of the hobbit Bilbo Baggins in another great fantasy: '*Baggins*: we hates it to pieces.'

Toto: that little yapping hairpiece of a creature, that meddlesome rug! (I should point out that I felt this way about Toto even when I still had hair of my own.) L. Frank Baum, excellent fellow, gave the dog a distinctly minor role: it kept Dorothy happy, and when she was not, it had a tendency to 'whine dismally': not an endearing trait. Its only really important contribution to the narrative of Baum's story came when it accidentally knocked over the screen behind which the Wizard stood concealed. The film-Toto rather more deliberately pulls aside a curtain to reveal the Great Humbug, and in spite of everything I found this an irritating piece of mischief-making. I was not surprised to learn that the canine actor playing Toto was possessed of a star's temperament, and even, at one point in the shooting, brought things to a standstill by staging a nervous breakdown. That Toto should be the film's one true object of love has always rankled. Useless (though satisfying) to protest: nobody, now, can rid me of this turbulent toupée.

....

When I first saw *The Wizard of Oz* it made a writer of me. Many years later, I began to devise the yarn that eventually became *Haroun and the Sea of Stories*, and felt strongly that if I could strike the right note it should be possible to write the tale in such a way as to make it of interest to adults as well as children: or, to use the phrase beloved of blurbists, to 'children from seven to seventy'. The world of books has become a severely categorized and demarcated affair, in which children's fiction is not only a kind of ghetto but one subdivided into writing for a number of different age groups. The cinema, however, has regularly risen above such categories. From Spielberg to Schwarzenegger, from Disney to Gilliam, it has come up with movies before which kids and adults sit side by side, united by what they are watching. I watched *Who Framed Roger Rabbit* in an afternoon cinema full of happily rowdy children, and went back to see it the next evening, at an hour too late for the kids, so that I could hear all the gags, enjoy the movie in-jokes, and marvel once more at the brilliance of the Toontown concept. But of all movies, the one that helped me most as I tried to find the right voice for *Haroun* was *The Wizard of Oz*. The film's traces are there in the text, plain to see; in Haroun's companions there are clear echoes of the friends who danced with Dorothy down the Yellow Brick Road.

And now I'm doing something strange, something that ought to destroy my love for the movie, but doesn't. Now I am watching a videotape, watching it with a notebook on my lap, a pen in one hand and a remote-control zapper in the other. I am subjecting *The Wizard of Oz* to the indignities of slow-motion, fast-forward and freeze-frame. I am trying to learn the secret of the magic trick. And, yes, I am seeing things I never noticed before...

... But I've changed too, of course. My own relationship with 'home' has become, let's say, more problematic of late, for reasons I have little interest in rehearsing here. I won't deny – and will amplify the admission in due course – that I've done a good deal of thinking, these past three years, about the advantages of a good pair of ruby slippers...

... The film begins. We are in the monochrome, 'real' world of Kansas. A girl and her dog run down a country lane. *She isn't coming yet, Toto. Did she hurt you? She tried to, didn't she?* A real girl, a real dog, and the beginning, with the very first line of dialogue, of real drama. Kansas, however, is not real, no more real than Oz. Kansas is an oil

Kansas

painting. Dorothy and Toto have been running down a short stretch of 'road' in the MGM studios, and this shot has been matted into a picture of emptiness. 'Real' emptiness would probably not be empty enough. It is as close as makes no difference to the universal grey of Frank Baum's story, the void broken only by a couple of fences and the vertical lines of telegraph poles. If Oz is *nowhere*, then the studio setting of the Kansas scenes suggests that *so is Kansas*. This is necessary. A realistic depiction of the extreme poverty of Dorothy Gale's circumstances would have created a burden, a heaviness, that would have rendered impossible the imaginative leap into Storyland, the soaring flight into Oz. The Grimms' fairytales, it's true, were often brutally realistic. In *The Fisherman and His Wife*, the eponymous couple live, until they meet the magic flounder, in what is tersely described as 'a pisspot'. But in many children's versions of the Grimms, the pisspot is bowdlerized into a 'hovel' or some even gentler word. Hollywood's vision has always been of this soft-focus variety. Dorothy looks extremely well-fed, and she is not really, but *unreally*, poor.

She arrives at the farmyard and here (freezing the frame) we see

Dorothy in the farmyard

the beginning of what will be a recurring visual motif. In the scene we have frozen, Dorothy and Toto are in the background, heading for a gate. To the left of the screen is a treetrunk, a vertical line echoing the telegraph poles of the scene before. Hanging from an approximately horizontal branch are a triangle and a circle (actually a rubber tyre). In midshot are further geometric elements: the parallel lines of the wooden fence, the bisecting diagonal wooden bar at the gate. Later, when we see the house, the theme of simple geometry is present once again; it is all right angles and triangles. The world of Kansas, that great void, is shaped into 'home' by the use of simple, uncomplicated shapes; none of your citified complexity here. Throughout *The Wizard of Oz*, home and safety are represented by such geometrical simplicity, whereas danger and evil are invariably twisty, irregular and misshapen.

The tornado is just such an untrustworthy, sinuous, shifting shape. Random, unfixed, it wrecks the plain shapes of that no-frills life.

Curiously, the Kansas sequence invokes not only geometry but arithmetic, too: for when Dorothy bursts upon Auntie Em and Uncle Henry with her fears about Toto, like the chaotic force she is, what are

The spiral of the Yellow Brick Road

they doing? Why do they shoo her away? 'We're trying to count,' they admonish her, as they take a census of eggs, counting their metaphorical chickens, their small hopes of income which the tornado will shortly blow away. So, with simple shapes and numbers, Dorothy's family erect their defences against the immense and maddening emptiness; and these defences are useless, of course.

Leaping ahead to Oz, it becomes obvious that this opposition between the geometric and the twisty is no accident. Look at the beginning of the Yellow Brick Road: it is a perfect spiral. Look again at Glinda's carriage, that perfect, luminous sphere. Look at the regimented routines of the Munchkins as they greet Dorothy and thank her for the death of the Wicked Witch of the East. Move on to the Emerald City: see it in the distance, its straight lines soaring into the sky! And now, by contrast, observe the Wicked Witch of the West: her crouching figure, her misshapen hat. How does she depart? In a puff of shapeless smoke... 'Only bad witches are ugly,' Glinda tells Dorothy, a remark of high Political Incorrectness that emphasizes the film's animosity towards whatever is tangled, claw-crooked, and weird. Woods are

The Witch departs in a puff of shapeless smoke

invariably frightening; the gnarled branches of trees are capable of coming to life; and the one moment when the Yellow Brick Road itself bewilders Dorothy is the moment when it ceases to be geometric (first spiral, then rectilinear) and splits and forks every which way.

. . . .

Back in Kansas, Auntie Em is delivering the scolding that is the prelude to one of the cinema's immortal moments. *You always get yourself into a fret about nothing ... find yourself a place where you won't get into any trouble!*

Some place where there isn't any trouble. Do you suppose there is such a place, Toto? There must be. Anybody who has swallowed the scriptwriters' notion that this is a film about the superiority of 'home' over 'away', that the 'moral' of *The Wizard of Oz* is as sickly-sweet as an embroidered sampler – 'East, West, home's best' – would do well to listen to the yearning in Judy Garland's voice, as her face tilts up towards the skies. What she expresses here, what she embodies with the purity of an archetype, is the human dream of *leaving*, a dream at least as powerful as its countervailing dream of roots. At the heart of *The Wizard of Oz* is a great tension between these two dreams; but as the music swells and that big, clean voice flies into the anguished longings of the song, can anyone doubt which message is the stronger? In its most potent emotional moment, this is unarguably a film about the joys of going away, of leaving the greyness and entering the colour, of making a new life in the 'place where there isn't any trouble'. 'Over the Rainbow' is, or ought to be, the anthem of all the world's migrants, all those who go in search of the place where 'the dreams that you dare to dream really do come true'. It is a celebration of Escape, a grand paean to the Uprooted Self, a hymn – *the* hymn – to Elsewhere.

E.Y. Harburg, the lyricist of 'Brother, Can You Spare A Dime?', and Harold Arlen, who had written 'It's Only A Paper Moon' with Harburg, made the songs for *The Wizard of Oz*, and Arlen actually did think of the melody line outside Schwab's drugstore in Hollywood. Aljean Harmetz records Harburg's disappointment with the music: too complex for a sixteen-year-old to sing, too advanced by comparison with Disney hits like 'Heigh Ho, Heigh Ho, It's Off To Work We Go'. Harmetz adds: 'To please Harburg, Arlen wrote the melody for the

tinkling middle section of the song.' *Where troubles melt like lemon drops, Away above the chimney tops, That's where you'll find me . . .* A little higher up, in short, than that other great ode to escape, 'Up On the Roof'.

That 'Over the Rainbow' came close to being cut out of the movie is well known, and proof positive that Hollywood makes its masterpieces by accident, because it simply does not know what it is doing. Other songs were dropped: 'The Jitter Bug', after five weeks' filming; and almost all of 'Lions and Tigers and Bears', which survives only as the chant of the Companions as they pass through the forest along the Yellow Brick Road:

> *Lions and tigers and bears – oh, my!*
> *Lions and tigers and bears – oh, my!*

It's impossible to say whether or not the film would have been improved or damaged by the addition of these songs; would *Catch-22* be *Catch-22* if it had been published under its original title of *Catch-18*? What is certain, however, is that Yip Harburg was wrong about Judy Garland's voice.

The leading actors in the cast complained that 'there was no acting' in the movie, and in the conventional sense they were correct. But Garland singing 'Over the Rainbow' did something extraordinary: in that moment she gave the film its heart, and the force of her rendition is strong and sweet and deep enough to carry us through all the tomfoolery that follows, even to bestow upon it a touching quality, a vulnerable charm, that is increased only by Bert Lahr's equally extraordinary creation of the role of the Cowardly Lion.

What is left to say about Garland's Dorothy? The conventional wisdom is that it gains in ironic force because its innocence contrasts so starkly with what we know of the actress's difficult later life. I'm not sure this is right, though it's the kind of remark movie buffs are prone to make. It seems to me that Garland's performance succeeds on its own terms and on the film's. She is required to pull off what sounds like an impossible trick. On the one hand she is to be the film's *tabula rasa*, the blank slate upon which the action of the story gradually writes itself – or, because it is a movie I'm discussing, the screen upon which the action plays. Armed only with a look of wide-eyed innocence, she must be the object of the film as much as its subject, must allow herself to be the empty vessel that the movie slowly fills. And yet, at the same time, she must (with a little help from the Cowardly Lion) carry the entire emotional weight, the whole cyclonic force, of the film. That she achieves this is due not only to the mature depths of her singing voice, but also to the odd stockiness, the gaucherie that endears us precisely because it is half-unbeautiful, *jolie-laide*, instead of the posturing beauty a Shirley Temple would have brought to the role – and Temple was certainly considered for the part. The scrubbed, ever so slightly lumpy *unsexiness* of Garland's playing is what makes the movie work. One can imagine the disastrous flirtatiousness young Shirley would have insisted on employing, and be grateful, once again, for the luck that persuaded the MGM executives to go with Judy.

The tornado that I've suggested is the product of the Gale in Dorothy's name and nature was actually made of muslin stiffened with wire. A props man was required to lower himself down into the muslin funnel to help pull the needles through and push them out again. 'It was pretty uncomfortable when we reached the narrow part,' he confessed. The tornado, swooping down on Dorothy's home, creates the second genuinely mythic image of *The Wizard of Oz*: the archetypal myth, one might say, of moving house.

In this, the transitional sequence of the movie, when the unreal reality of Kansas gives way to the realistic surreality of the world of wizardry, there is, as befits a threshold moment, much business involving windows and doors. First, the farmhands open up the doors of the storm shelter, and Uncle Henry, heroic as ever, persuades Auntie Em that they can't afford to wait for Dorothy. Second, Dorothy, returning with Toto from her attempt at running away, struggles against the wind to open the screen door of the main house; this outer door is instantly ripped from its hinges and blows away. Third, we see the others closing the doors of the storm shelter. Fourth, Dorothy, inside the house, opens and shuts the doors of various rooms, calling out frantically for Auntie Em. Fifth, Dorothy goes to the storm shelter, but its doors are locked against her. Sixth, Dorothy retreats back inside the main house, her cries for Auntie Em now weak and fearful; whereupon a window, echoing the screen door, blows off its hinges and knocks her cold. She falls upon the bed, and from now on magic reigns. We have passed through the film's most important gateway.

Much business involving
windows and doors:
The farmhands open up the
doors

The doors of the storm shelter
close

Dorothy calls out for
Auntie Em

The doors are locked against Dorothy

A window knocks Dorothy cold

She falls upon the bed

But this device – the knocking-out of Dorothy – is the most radical and in some ways the worst of all the changes wrought in Frank Baum's original conception. For in the book *there is no question that Oz is real*, that it is a place of the same order, though not of the same type, as Kansas. The film, like the TV soap opera *Dallas*, introduces an element of bad faith when it permits the possibility that everything that follows is a dream. This type of bad faith cost *Dallas* its audience and eventually killed it off. That *The Wizard of Oz* avoided the soap opera's fate is a testament to the general integrity of the film, which enabled it to transcend this hoary, creaking cliché.

While the house flies through the air, looking in long-shot like a tiny toy, Dorothy 'awakes'. What she sees through the window is a sort of movie – the window acting as a cinema-screen, a frame within the frame – which prepares her for the new sort of movie she is about to step into. The effect shots, sophisticated for their time, include a lady knitting in her rocking chair as the tornado whirls her by, a cow placidly standing in the eye of the storm, two men rowing a boat through the twisting air, and, most important of all, the figure of Miss Gulch on her bicycle, which transforms, as we watch it, into the figure of the Wicked Witch of the West on her broomstick, her cape flying behind her, and her huge cackling laugh rising above the storm.

....

The house lands; Dorothy emerges from her bedroom with Toto in her arms. We have reached the moment of colour.

The first colour shot, in which Dorothy walks away from the camera towards the front door of the house, is deliberately dull, an attempt to match the preceding monochrome. But once the door is open, colour floods the screen. In these colour-glutted days it's hard to imagine ourselves back in a time when colour was still relatively new in the movies. Thinking back once again to my Bombay childhood in the 1950s, a time when Hindi movies were *all* in black-and-white, I can recall the excitement of the advent of colour. It was in an epic about the Grand Mughal, the Emperor Akbar, entitled *Mughal-e-Azam*, and there was only one reel of colour photography, featuring a dance at court by the fabled Anarkali. Yet this reel alone guaranteed the film's success, drawing the crowds in their millions.

The window acting as a
cinema screen
A lady knitting

A cow standing in the eye of
the storm

Two men in a boat

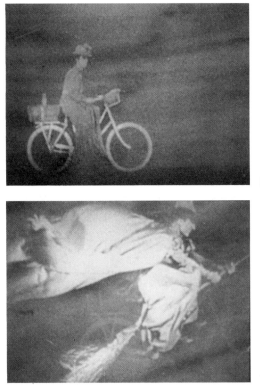

Miss Gulch

The Wicked Witch of the West

The makers of *The Wizard of Oz* clearly decided that they were going to make their colour as colourful as possible, much as Michelangelo Antonioni (a very different sort of film-maker) did, years later, in his first colour feature *The Red Desert*. In the Antonioni film colour is used to create heightened and often surrealistic effects. *The Wizard of Oz* likewise goes for bold, expressionist splashes – the yellow of the Brick Road, the red of the Poppy Field, the green of the Emerald City and of the witch's skin. So striking were these colour effects that, soon after seeing the film as a child, I began to dream of green-skinned witches; years afterwards, I gave these dreams to the narrator of my novel *Midnight's Children*, having completely forgotten their source. 'No colours except green and black the walls are green the sky is black . . . the stars are green the Widow is green but her hair is black as black,' begins the stream-of-consciousness dream-sequence, in which the nightmare of Indira Gandhi is fused with the equally nightmarish figure of Margaret Hamilton: a coming-together of the Wicked Witches of the East and of the West.

Dorothy, stepping into colour, framed by exotic foliage with a cluster of dwarfy cottages behind her and looking like a blue-smocked Snow White, no princess but a good demotic American gal, is clearly struck by the absence of her familiar homey grey. *Toto, I have a feeling we're not in Kansas any more*, she says, and that camp classic of a line has detached itself from the movie to become a great American catchphrase, endlessly recycled, even turning up as one of the epigraphs to Thomas Pynchon's mammoth paranoid fantasy of World War II, *Gravity's Rainbow*, whose characters' destiny lies not 'Behind the moon, beyond the rain', but 'beyond the zero' of consciousness, where lies a land at least as bizarre as Oz.

But Dorothy has done more than step out of the grey into Technicolor. Her homelessness, her *unhousing*, is underlined by the fact that, after all the door-play of the transitional sequence, and having now stepped out of doors, she will not be permitted to enter any interior at all until she arrives at the Emerald City. From Tornado to Wizard, Dorothy never has a roof over her head.

Out there amid the giant hollyhocks, which bear blooms like old gramophone trumpets, there in the vulnerability of open space (albeit open space that isn't at all like the prairie), Dorothy is about to outdo

Snow White by a factor of about fifty. You can almost hear the MGM studio chiefs plotting to put the Disney hit in the shade; not simply by providing in live-action almost as many miraculous effects as the Disney cartoonists, but also in the matter of the little people. If Snow White had seven dwarfs, the studio bosses decided, then Dorothy Gale, from the star called Kansas, would have three hundred and fifty.

There is some disagreement about how this many Munchkins were located, brought to Hollywood and signed up. Aljean Harmetz's book gives the official version, that they were provided by an impresario named Leo Singer; but John Lahr's biography of his father Bert tells a different tale, which I prefer to give here for reasons Roger Rabbit would understand: i.e., only because it is funny. Lahr quotes the film's casting director, Bill Grady:

> Leo (Singer) could only give me 150. I went to a midget monologist called Major Doyle . . . I said I had 150 from Singer.
>
> 'I'll not give you one if you do business with that son-of-a-bitch.' 'What am I gonna do?' I said. 'I'll get you the 350.' . . . So I called up Leo and explained the situation . . . When I told the Major that I'd called off Singer, he danced a jig right on the street in front of Dinty Moore's.
>
> The Major gets these midgets for me . . . I bring them out West in buses . . . Major Doyle took the (first three) buses and arrived at Singer's house.
>
> The Major went to the doorman. 'Phone upstairs and tell Leo Singer to look out the window.'
>
> It took about ten minutes. Then Singer looked from his fifth-floor window. And there were all those midgets in those buses in front of his house with their bare behinds sticking out the window.

This incident became known as 'Major Doyle's Revenge'.

What began with a strip continued in cartoon style. The Munchkins were made up and costumed exactly like 3D cartoon figures. The Mayor of Munchkinland is quite implausibly rotund; the Coroner (*and she's not only merely dead/She's really most sincerely dead*) reads the Witch of the East's obituary from a scroll while wearing a hat with an absurdly scroll-like brim; the quiffs of the Lollipop Kids, who

The Munchkins:
The Mayor

The Coroner

The Sleepy Heads

The Lullaby League

The Lollipop Kids

appear to have arrived in Oz by way of Bash Street and Dead End, stand up more stiffly than Tintin's. But what might have been a grotesque and unappetizing sequence in fact becomes the moment in which *The Wizard of Oz* captures its audience once and for all, by allying the natural charm of the story to brilliant MGM choreography (which alternates large-scale routines with neat little set-pieces like the dance of the Lullaby League and the Sleepy Heads awaking mob-capped and be-nightied out of cracked blue eggshells set in a giant nest), and above all through Arlen and Harburg's exceptionally witty 'Ding, Dong, the Witch is Dead'.

Arlen was a little contemptuous of this song and the equally unforgettable 'We're Off to See the Wizard', calling them his 'lemon-drop songs', and perhaps this is because the real inventiveness in both tunes lies in Harburg's lyrics. In Dorothy's intro to 'Ding, Dong', Harburg embarked on a pyrotechnic display of A-A-A rhymes (*the wind began to switch/the house to pitch*; until at length we meet the *witch/a-thumbin' for a hitch*; and *what happened then was rich* . . .), a series in which, as with a vaudeville barker's alliterations, we cheer each new rhyme as a sort of gymnastic triumph. This type of verbal play continues to characterize both songs. In 'Ding, Dong', Harburg begins to invent punning, concertinaed words:

> Ding, Dong, the witch is dead!
> *Whicholwitch?*
> – The wicked witch!

And this technique found much fuller expression in 'We're Off to See the Wizard', becoming the real 'hook' of the song:

> We're off to see the Wizard
> The wonderful *Wizzerdevoz*;
> We hear he is
> A *Wizzavawizz*,
> If ever a *Wizztherwozz*.
> If *everoever* a *Wizztherwozz*
> The *Wizzerdevoz* is one because . . .

And so on. Is it too fanciful to suggest that Harburg's use throughout the film of a rhyme-scheme much enamoured of internal rhymes and assonances is a conscious echo of the 'rhyming' of the plot itself, the paralleling of characters in Kansas with those in Oz, the echoes of themes bouncing back and forth between the monochrome and Technicolor worlds?

Few of the Munchkins could actually sing their lines, as they didn't speak English (the songs had to be post-synched). They weren't actually required to do much in the movie. They made up for this by their activities off-camera, and though some film historians nowadays try to play down the legends of carousing, sexual shenanigans and general mayhem, the legend of the Munchkin hordes cutting a swathe through Hollywood will not lie down easily. In Angela Carter's novel *Wise Children* there is a wild comic account of a fictitious Hollywood version of *A Midsummer Night's Dream* that owes a good deal to the Munchkins:

> The concept of this wood was scaled to the size of fairy folk, so all was twice as large as life. Larger. Daisies big as your head and white as spooks, foxgloves as tall as the tower of Pisa that chimed like bells if shook . . . Even the wee folk were real; the studio scoured the country for dwarfs. Soon, true or not, wild tales began to circulate – how one poor chap fell into the toilet and splashed around for half an hour before someone dashed in for a piss and fished him out of the bowl; another one got offered a highchair in the Brown Derby when he went out for a hamburger . . .

and, one might add, there were incidents involving knives, and passions developed by this or that Munchkin for larger employees of the studio.

Amidst all this Munchkining, we are given two very different portraits of adults. The Good Witch Glinda is pretty in pink (well, prettyish, even if Dorothy is moved to call her 'beautiful'). She has a high, cooing elocution voice, and a smile that seems to have jammed. She has one excellent gag-line, after Dorothy disclaims witchy status: pointing at Toto, Glinda enquires, *Well then, is* that *the witch?* This joke apart, she spends the scene simpering and looking generally benevolent and loving and rather too heavily powdered. Interestingly, though she is the Good Witch, the goodness of Oz does not inhere in her. The people of Oz are naturally good, unless they are under the power of the

Above: The Good Witch Glinda
Below: The Wicked Witch of the West

Wicked Witch (as is shown by the improved behaviour of the Witch's soldiers after the Witch melts). In the moral universe of the film, then, only evil is external, dwelling solely in the dual devil-figure of Miss Gulch/Wicked Witch.

(A parenthetical worry about the presentation of Munchkinland: is it not a mite too pretty, too kempt, too sweetly sweet for a place that was, until moments before Dorothy's arrival, under the absolute power of the evil and dictatorial Witch of the East? How is it that this squashed Witch had no castle? How could her despotism have left so little mark upon the land? Why are the Munchkins so relatively unafraid, hiding only briefly before they emerge, and giggling while they hide? The heretical thought occurs: maybe the Witch of the East *wasn't as bad as all that* – she certainly kept the streets clean, the houses painted and in good repair, and no doubt such trains as there might be, running on time. Moreover, and again unlike her sister, she seems to have ruled without the aid of soldiers, policemen or other regiments of repression. Why, then, was she so hated? I only ask.)

Glinda and the Witch of the West are the only two symbols of power in a film which is largely about the powerless, and it's instructive to 'unpack' them. They are both women, and a striking aspect of *The Wizard of Oz* is its lack of a male hero – because, for all their brains, heart and courage, it is impossible to see the Scarecrow, Tin Man and Cowardly Lion as classic Hollywood leading men. The power centre of the film is a triangle at whose points are Glinda, Dorothy and the Witch; the fourth point, at which the Wizard is thought for most of the film to stand, turns out to be an illusion. The power of men, it is suggested, is illusory; the power of women is real.

Of the two Witches, good and bad, can there be anyone who'd choose to spend five minutes with Glinda? The actress who played her, Billie Burke, the ex-wife of Flo Ziegfeld, sounds every bit as wimpy as her role; she was prone to react to criticism with a trembling lip and a faltering cry of 'Oh, you're *browbeating* me!' Margaret Hamilton's Wicked Witch of the West, by contrast, seizes hold of the film from her very first, green-faced snarl.

Of course Glinda is 'good' and the Wicked Witch 'bad'; but Glinda is a trilling pain in the neck, and the Wicked Witch is lean and mean. Check out their clothes: frilly pink versus slimline black. *No contest.* Consider their attitudes to their fellow-women: Glinda simpers upon being called beautiful, and denigrates her unbeautiful sisters; whereas the Wicked Witch is in a rage because of the death of her sister, demonstrating, one might say, a commendable sense of solidarity. We may hiss at her, and she may terrify us as children, but at least she doesn't embarrass us the way Glinda does. It's true that Glinda does exude a sort of raddled motherly safeness, while the Witch of the West looks, in this scene anyhow, curiously frail and impotent, obliged to mouth empty threats – *I'll bide my time. But you just try and keep out of my way* – but just as feminism has sought to rehabilitate pejorative old words such as hag, crone, witch, so the Wicked Witch of the West could be said to represent the more positive of the two images of powerful womanhood on offer here.

Glinda and the Wicked Witch clash most fiercely over the ruby slippers, which Glinda magicks off the feet of the dead Witch of the East and on to Dorothy's feet, and which the Wicked Witch seemingly has no powers to remove. But Glinda's instructions to Dorothy are oddly enigmatic, even contradictory. She tells Dorothy (1) 'Their magic must be very powerful or she wouldn't want them so badly', and, later, (2) 'Never let those ruby slippers off your feet or you will be at the mercy of the Wicked Witch of the West.' Now, statement (1) suggests that Glinda is unclear about the nature of the ruby slippers, whereas statement (2) suggests that she knows all about their protective power. Nor does either statement hint at the ruby slippers' later role in helping to get Dorothy back to Kansas. It seems probable that these confusions are hangovers from the long, dissension-riddled scripting process, in which the function of the slippers was the subject of considerable dispute. But one can also see Glinda's obliquities as proof that a good fairy or a good witch, when she sets out to be of assistance, never gives you everything. Glinda is not so unlike her description of the Wizard of Oz, after all: *Oh, he's very good, but very mysterious.*

. . . .

Just follow the Yellow Brick Road, says Glinda, and bubbles off into the blue remembered hills in the distance, and Dorothy, geometrically influenced as who would not be after a childhood among triangles, circles and squares, begins her journey at the very point from which the Road spirals outwards. And as she does so, and while both she and the Munchkins echo Glinda's instructions in tones both raucously high and gutturally low, something begins to happen to her feet; their motion acquires a syncopation, which by beautifully slow stages grows more and more noticeable; until at last, as the ensemble bursts for the first time into the film's theme song – *You're off to see the Wizard*, they sing – we see, fully developed, the clever, shuffling little skip that will be the leitmotif of the entire journey:

> *You're off to see the Wizard*
>   (s-skip)
> *The wonderful Wizzerdevoz*
>   (s-skip)
> *We hear he is a Wizzavawizz*
> *If ever a Wizztherwoz...*

In this way, s-skipping along, Dorothy Gale, who is already a National Heroine of Munchkinland, who is already (as the Munchkins have assured her) History, who *will be a Bust in the Hall of Fame*, steps out along the road of destiny, and heads, as Americans must, into the West: towards the sunset, the Emerald City, and the Witch.

I have always found off-camera anecdotes about a film's production simultaneously delicious and disappointing, especially when the film has lodged as deep down inside as *The Wizard of Oz*. On the one hand there's an undeniable Trivial Pursuitish hunger to be satisfied: did you know that Buddy Ebsen (later the patriarch of the Beverly Hillbillies) was the original Scarecrow, then switched roles with Ray Bolger, who didn't want to play the Tin Man? And did you know that Ebsen had to leave the film after his costume gave him asbestos poisoning? And did you know that Margaret Hamilton's hand was badly burned during the filming of the scene in which the Witch writes SURRENDER DOROTHY in the sky over the Emerald City, and that her stunt double Betty Danko was even more badly burned during the reshoot of this scene? And did you know that Jack Haley (the third and final choice for Tin Man) couldn't sit down in his costume and could only rest against a specially devised 'leaning board'? That none of the three leading men were allowed to eat their meals in the MGM refectory because their make-up was thought too revolting? That Margaret Hamilton was given a coarse tent instead of a proper changing room, as if she really were a witch? That Bert Lahr would sweat, inside his suit, more like a pig than a lion? That Toto was a female and her real name was Terry? Above all, did you know that the frock-coat worn by Frank Morgan, playing Professor Marvel/the Wizard of Oz, was bought from a second-hand store, bore the name of – and was afterwards proven to have been made for – the author himself, L. Frank Baum?

What is sad about many such tales is the revelation that the experience of making a film bears more or less no relationship to the experience of watching it. It is almost certainly untrue that Haley, Bolger and Lahr were unkind to Judy Garland, as some stories say, but Margaret Hamilton definitely felt excluded by the boys. She was lonely on set, her studio days barely coinciding at all with the one actor she already knew, Frank Morgan, and she couldn't even take a leak without assistance. The point is that hardly anyone – certainly not Lahr, Haley and Bolger in their elaborate make-up, which they dreaded putting on every day – seems to have had any fun in the making of one of the most enjoyable pictures in movie history. We do not really want to know this; and yet, so fatally willing are we to do that which may destroy our illusions, that we also do want to know, we do, we do.

And so, as I delved into the secrets of the Wizard of Oz's drinking problem, and learned that Morgan was only third choice for the part, behind W.C. Fields and Ed Wynn, and as I wondered what contemptuous wildness Fields might have brought to the role, and how it might have been if his female more-than-opposite number, the Witch, had been played by the first choice, Gale Sondergaard, not only a great beauty but also another Gale to set alongside Dorothy and the tornado, I found myself staring at an old colour photograph of the Scarecrow, the Tin Man and Dorothy, posing in a forest set, surrounded by autumn leaves; and realized that I was not looking at the stars at all, but at their stunt doubles, their stand-ins. It was an unremarkable studio still, but it took my breath away; for it, too, was both melancholy and mesmeric. In my mind, it came to be the very epitome of the doubleness of my responses.

There they stand, Nathanael West's locusts, the ultimate

wannabes. Garland's shadow, Bobbie Koshay, with her hands clasped behind her back and a white bow in her hair, is doing her brave best to smile, but she knows she's a counterfeit all right; there are no ruby slippers on her feet. The mock-Scarecrow looks glum, too, even though he has avoided the full-scale burlap-sack make-up that was Bolger's daily fate. If it were not for the clump of straw poking out of his right sleeve, you'd think he was some kind of hobo. Between them, in full metallic drag, stands the Tin Man's tinnier echo, looking as miserable as hell. Stand-ins know their fate: they know we don't want to admit their existence. Even when our rational minds tell us that in this or that difficult shot – when the Witch flies, when the Cowardly Lion dives through a glass window – we aren't watching the stars, yet the part of us that has suspended disbelief insists on seeing the stars and not their doubles. Thus the stand-ins are rendered invisible even when they are in full view. They remain off-camera even when they are on-screen.

However, this is not the reason for the curious fascination of the photograph, which arises from the fact that, in the case of a beloved film, *we are all the stars' doubles.* Our imaginations put us in the Lion's skin, place the sparkling slippers on our feet, and send us cackling through the air on a broomstick. To look at this photograph is to look into a mirror; in it we see ourselves. The world of *The Wizard of Oz* has possessed us. We are the stand-ins now.

A pair of ruby slippers, found in a bin in the MGM basement, was sold at auction in May 1970 for the amazing sum of $15,000. The purchaser was, and has remained, anonymous. Who was it who wished so profoundly to possess, perhaps even to wear, Dorothy's magic shoes? Was it, dear reader, you? Was it I?

At the same auction the second highest price was paid for the Cowardly Lion's costume ($2,400). This was twice as much as the next largest bid, $1,200 for Clark Gable's trench-coat. The high prices earned by *Wizard of Oz* memorabilia testify to the power of the film over its admirers, to our desire, quite literally, to clothe ourselves in its raiment. The story of the auction of the ruby slippers has been fictionalized and retold in Part II of this book, but there is one irony that is entirely non-fictional. After the auction, it was suggested that the $15,000 slippers were too large to have fitted Judy Garland's feet. They had, in all probability, been made for her double, Bobbie Koshay, whose feet were two sizes larger. Is it not fitting that the shoes made for the stand-in to stand in should have passed into the possession of another form of surrogate: a film fan?

....

If asked to pick a single defining image of *The Wizard of Oz*, most of us would, I suspect, come up with the Scarecrow, the Tin Man, the Cowardly Lion and Dorothy s-skipping down the Yellow Brick Road (in point of fact, the skip continues to grow throughout the journey, becoming a full-fledged h-hop). How strange that the most famous passage of this very *filmic* film, a film packed with technical wizardry and effects, should be by some distance the least cinematic, the most 'stagey' part of the whole! Or perhaps not so strange, for this is primarily a passage of surreal comedy, and we recall that the equally inspired clowning of the Marx Brothers was no less stagily filmed; the zany mayhem of the playing made any but the simplest camera techniques impossible.

Skipping down the Yellow Brick Road

'Where is Vaudeville?' Somewhere on the way to the Wizard, apparently. The Scarecrow and the Tin Man are pure products of the burlesque theatre, specializing in pantomime exaggerations of voice and body movements, pratfalls (the Scarecrow descending from his post), improbable leanings beyond the centre of gravity (the Tin Man during his little dance), and, of course, the smartass backchat of the crosstalk act:

> TIN MAN, *rusted solid*: (Squawks)
> DOROTHY: He said 'Oil can'!
> SCARECROW: Oil can what?

At the pinnacle of all this clowning is that fully-realized comic masterpiece of a creation: Bert Lahr's Cowardly Lion, all elongated vowel sounds (*Put 'em uuuuuuuup*), ridiculous rhymes (*rhinoceros/ imposserous*), transparent bravado and huge, operatic, tail-tugging, blubbing terror. All three, Scarecrow, Tin Man and Lion, are, in Eliot's phrase, hollow men. The Scarecrow, of course, actually does have a 'headpiece filled with straw, alas!'; but the Tin Man, the ancestor of See

Threepio in *Star Wars*, is no less empty – he even bangs on his chest to prove that his innards are missing, because 'the Tinsmith', his shadowy Maker, forgot to provide a heart; and the Lion lacks the most leonine of qualities, lamenting:

> What makes the Hottentot so hot,
> What puts the ape in apricot,
> What have they got that I ain't got?
> Courage!

Perhaps it is because they are all hollow that our imaginations can enter them and fill them up so easily. That is to say, it is their anti-heroism, their apparent lack of Great Qualities, that makes them our size, or even smaller, so that we can stand amongst them as equals, like Dorothy among the Munchkins. Gradually, however, we discover that, along with their 'straight man', Dorothy (who occupies in this sequence the role of the unfunny Marx Brother, the one who could sing and look hunky and do little else), they embody one of the film's 'messages' – that we already possess what we seek most fervently. The Scarecrow

regularly comes up with bright ideas, which he offers with self-deprecating disclaimers. The Tin Man can weep with grief long before the Wizard gives him a heart. And Dorothy's capture by the Witch brings out the Lion's courage, even though he pleads with his friends to 'talk me out of it'.

For this message to have its full impact, however, it is necessary that we learn the futility of looking for solutions *outside*. We must learn about one more hollow man: the Wizard of Oz himself. Just as the Tinsmith was a flawed Maker of Tin Men – just as, in this secular movie, the Tin Man's god is dead – so too must our belief in wizards perish, so that we may believe in ourselves. We must survive the Deadly Poppy Field, helped by a mysterious snowfall (why *does* snow overcome the poppies' poison?), and so arrive, accompanied by heavenly choirs, at the city gates.

. . . .

Here the film changes convention once again, becoming a portrait of hicks from the sticks arriving at the metropolis, one of the classic

themes of American films, with echoes in *Mr Deeds Goes to Town*, or even in Clark Kent's arrival at the *Daily Planet* in *Superman.* Dorothy is a country hick, *Dorothy the small and meek*; her companions are backwoods buffoons. Yet – and this, too, is a familiar Hollywood trope – it is the out-of-towners, the country mice, who will save the day.

There was never a metropolis quite like Emerald City, however. It looks from the outside like a fairy-tale of New York, a thicket of sky-scraping green towers. On the inside, though, it's the very essence of quaintness. Even more startling is the discovery that the citizens – many of them played by Frank Morgan, who adds the parts of the gatekeeper, the driver of the horse-drawn buggy and the palace guard to those of Professor Marvel and the Wizard – speak with what Hollywood actors like to call an English accent. *Tyke yer any place in the city, we does*, says the coachman, adding *I'll tyke yer to a little place where you can tidy up a bit, what?* Other members of the citizenry are dressed like Grand Hotel bellhops and glitzy nuns, and they say, or rather sing, things, like *Jolly good fun!* Dorothy catches on quickly. At the Wash and Brush Up, a tribute to urban technological genius with none of the dark doubts of a *Modern Times* or a *City Lights*, our heroine gets a little Englished herself:

> DOROTHY (sings): Can you even dye my eyes
> to match my gown?
> ATTENDANTS (in unison): Uh-huh!
> DOROTHY: Jolly old town!

Most of the citizenry are cheerfully friendly, and those that appear not to be – the gatekeeper, the palace guard – are soon won over. (In this respect, once again, they are untypical city folk.) Our four friends finally gain entry to the Wizard's palace because Dorothy's tears of frustration un-dam a quite alarming reservoir of liquid in the guard, whose face is soon sodden with tears, and watching this extreme performance you are struck by the sheer number of occasions on which people cry in this film. Apart from Dorothy and the guard, there is the Cowardly Lion, who bawls when Dorothy bops him on the nose; the aforementioned Tin Man, who almost rusts up again from weeping; and Dorothy again, while in the clutches of the Witch. It occurs to you that if the Witch could only have been closer at hand on one of these occasions, the movie might have been much shorter.

Into the palace we go, down an arched corridor that looks like an elongated version of the Looney Tunes logo, and at last we confront a Wizard whose illusions of giant heads and flashes of fire conceal (but only for a while) his basic kinship with Dorothy. He, too, is an immigrant; indeed, as he will later reveal, he is a Kansas man himself. (In the novel, he came from Omaha.) These two immigrants have adopted opposite strategies of survival in a new and strange land. Dorothy has been unfailingly polite, careful, courteously 'small and meek', whereas the Wizard has been fire and smoke, bravado and bombast, and has hustled his way to the top, floated there, so to speak, on a cloud of his own hot air. But Dorothy learns that meekness isn't enough, and the Wizard finds (as his balloon gets the better of him for a second time) that his command of hot air isn't all it should be. It is hard for a migrant like myself not to see in these shifting destinies a parable of the migrant condition.

The Wizard's stipulation, that he will grant no wishes until the four friends have brought him the Witch's broomstick, usher in the penultimate and least challenging (though most action-packed and

The Wizard's Palace

'exciting') movement of the film, which is in this phase at once a buddy movie, a straightforward adventure yarn and, after Dorothy's capture, a more or less conventional Princess Rescue Story. The film, having arrived at the great dramatic climax of the confrontation with the Wizard of Oz, sags for a while, and doesn't really regain momentum until the equally climactic final struggle with the Wicked Witch of the West, ending with her melting, her 'growing down' into nothingness. The relative dullness of this sequence has much to do with the script's inability to make anything of the Winged Monkeys, who remain ciphers throughout, whereas they could have been used (for example) to show us what the Munchkins might have been like before their liberation by Dorothy's falling house.

. . . .

One interesting detail. The Witch, dispatching the Winged Monkeys to capture Dorothy, speaks a line that makes no sense at all. Assuring the chief Monkey that his prey will give him no trouble, the Witch adds: *I've sent a little insect on ahead to take the fight out of them.* But, as we cut down to the forest, we learn nothing at all about such an insect. There is simply no such insect in the film. There was, though; this line of dialogue is a hangover from an earlier version of the film, and it refers to the ghost of the excised musical sequence I mentioned earlier. The 'little insect' was once a fully fledged song, that took over a month to film. He is the Jitter Bug.

. . . .

Fast-forward. The Witch is gone. The Wizard has been unmasked, and in the moment of his unveiling has succeeded in a spot of true magic, giving Dorothy's companions the gifts they did not believe they possessed until that moment. The Wizard has gone, too, and without Dorothy, their plans having been fouled up by (who else but) Toto. And here is Glinda, telling Dorothy she had to learn the meaning of the ruby slippers for herself...

GLINDA: What have you learned?

DOROTHY: If I ever go looking for my heart's desire again, I won't look further than my own back yard. And if it isn't there, I never really lost it to begin with. Is that right?

GLINDA: That's all it is. And now those magic slippers will take you home in two seconds.

... Close your eyes ... click your heels together three times ... and think to yourself ... there's no place like ...

Hold it.
Hold *it*.

How does it come about, at the close of this radical and enabling film, which teaches us in the least didactic way possible to build on what we have, to make the best of ourselves, that we are given this conservative little homily? Are we to believe that Dorothy has learned no more on her journey than that she didn't need to make such a journey in the first

place? Must we accept that she now accepts the limitations of her home life, and agrees that the things she doesn't have there are no loss to her? *Is that right?*' Well, excuse *me*, Glinda, but is it hell.

Home again in black-and-white, with Auntie Em and Uncle Henry and the rude mechanicals clustered round her bed, Dorothy begins her second revolt, fighting not only against the patronizing dismissals of her own folk but also against the scriptwriters, and the sentimental moralizing of the entire Hollywood studio system. *It wasn't a dream, it was a place*, she cries piteously. *A real, truly live place! Doesn't anyone believe me?*

Many, many people did believe her. Frank Baum's readers believed her, and their interest in Oz led him to write thirteen further Oz books, admittedly of diminishing quality; the series was continued, even more feebly, by other hands after his death. Dorothy, ignoring the 'lessons' of the ruby slippers, went back to Oz, in spite of the efforts of Kansas folk, including Auntie Em and Uncle Henry, to have her dreams brainwashed out of her (see the terrifying electro-convulsive therapy sequence in the recent Disney film *Return to Oz*); and, in the sixth book of the series, she took Auntie Em and Uncle Henry with her, and they all settled down in Oz, where Dorothy became a Princess.

So Oz finally *became* home; the imagined world became the actual world, as it does for us all, because the truth is that once we have left our childhood places and started out to make up our lives, armed only with what we have and are, we understand that the real secret of the ruby slippers is not that 'there's no place like home', but rather that there is no longer any such place *as* home: except, of course, for the home we make, or the homes that are made for us, in Oz: which is anywhere, and everywhere, except the place from which we began.

II
AT THE AUCTION OF THE RUBY SLIPPERS

The bidders who have assembled for the auction of the magic slippers bear little resemblance to your usual saleroom crowd. The Auctioneers have publicized the event widely and are prepared for all comers. People venture out but rarely nowadays; nevertheless, and rightly, the Auctioneers believed this prize would tempt us from our bunkers. High feelings are anticipated, and accordingly, in addition to the standard facilities provided for the comfort and security of the more notable personages, extra-large bronze cuspidors have been placed in the toilets, for the use of the physically sick, and psychiatrists of differing disciplines have been installed in strategically located neo-Gothic confessional booths, to counsel the sick at heart.

Most of us nowadays are sick.

There are no priests; the Auctioneers have drawn a line. The priests remain in other, nearby buildings, buildings with which they are familiar, hoping to deal with any psychic fallout, any insanity overspill.

Units of obstetricians and helmeted police SWAT teams wait out of sight in side alleys in case the excitement leads to unexpected births or deaths. Lists of next of kin have been drawn up and their contact numbers recorded. A supply of straitjackets has been laid in.

See: behind bullet-proof glass, the ruby slippers sparkle. Movie stars are here, among the bidders, bringing their glossy, spangled auras to the saleroom. When one of us collides with a star's priceless (and fragile) aura, he or she is instantly knocked to the floor by a security team and hustled out to the waiting paddy-wagons. Such incidents slightly reduce the crush in the Grand Saleroom.

The memorabilia junkies are out in predictable force, and now with a ducking movement of the head one of them applies her desperate lips to the slippers' transparent cage, setting off the state-of-the-art alarm system whose programmers have neglected to teach it about the relative harmlessness of such an osculation. The alarm system pumps a hundred thousand volts of electricity into the silicon-implanted lips of the glass kisser, terminating her interest in proceedings. It is an unpleasantly whiffy moment, but it fails to deter a second aficionado from the same suicidal kissery. When we learn that this crazed moron was the lover of the first fatality, we wonder rather at the mysteries of love, whilst reaching once again for our perfumed handkerchiefs.

A fancy-dress party is in full swing. Wizards, Lions, Scarecrows are in plentiful supply. They jostle crossly for position, stamping on one another's feet. There is a scarcity of Tin Men on account of the particular discomfort of the costume. Witches bide their time on the *balcons* and *gallerias* of the Grand Saleroom, living gargoyles with, in many cases, high credit ratings. One corner is occupied entirely by Totos, several of whom are copulating enthusiastically, obliging a rubber-gloved janitor to separate them so as to avoid giving public offence. He does this with no little delicacy and taste.

We, the public, are easily, lethally offended.

Around the – let us say – shrine of the ruby-sequined slippers, pools of saliva have been forming. There are those of us who lack restraint, who drool. The jump-suited Latino janitor moves among us, a pail in one hand and a squeegee mop in the other. We admire and are grateful for his talent for self-effacement. He removes our mouth waters without causing any loss of face on our part.

Opportunities for encountering the miraculous are limited in our Nietzschean, relativistic universe. Behaviourist philosophers and quantum scientists crowd around the magic shoes.

Exiles, displaced persons of all sorts, even homeless tramps have turned up for a glimpse of the impossible, emerging from their subterranean hollows and braving the bazookas, the Uzi-armed gangs high on crack or ice, the smugglers, the emptiers of houses. The tramps wear stenchy jute ponchos and hawk noisily into the giant potted yuccas. They grab fistfuls of canapés from trays borne upon the superb palms of A-list caterers. Sushi is eaten by them with impressive quantities of *wasabi* sauce, to whose inflammatory powers the hoboes' innards seem impervious. SWAT teams are summoned and after a brief battle involving the use of rubber bullets and sedative darts the tramps are removed, clubbed into unconsciousness and driven away. They will be deposited some distance beyond the city limits, out there in that smoking no-man's land into which we venture no more. Wild dogs will gather around them, eager for lunch. These are uncompromising times.

Political refugees are at the auction: conspirators, deposed monarchs, defeated factions, poets, bandit chieftains. Such figures no longer wear the black berets, pebble-lensed spectacles and enfolding greatcoats of yesteryear, but strike resplendent attitudes in boxy silken jackets and high-waisted Japanese couture trousers. The women wear toreador jackets bearing sequined representations of great works of art. One beauty parades *Guernica* on her back, while several others wear glittering scenes from the *Disasters of War* sequence by Francisco Goya. Incandescent in their suits of lights, the female political refugees fail to eclipse the ruby slippers, and huddle with their male comrades in small hissing bunches, periodically hurling imprecations, ink-pellets, spitballs and paper darts across the salon at rival clusters of émigrés. The guards at the exits crack their bullwhips idly and the politicals control themselves.

Disapproving critiques of the fetishizing of the slippers are offered by religious fundamentalists, who have been allowed to gain entry by virtue of the extreme liberalism of some of the Auctioneers, who argue that a civilized Saleroom must be a broad church, open, tolerant. The fundamentalists have expressed their desire to buy the magic footwear in order to burn it, and this is not, in the view of the liberal Auctioneers, an unreasonable request. What price tolerance if the intolerant are not tolerated also? Money insists on democracy; anyone's cash is as good as anyone else's. The fundamentalists fulminate from their soap-boxes, and are ignored; but some senior figures present speak ominously of the thin end of the wedge.

Orphans arrive, hoping that the ruby slippers might transport them back through time as well as space, and reunite them with their deceased parents. There is even a baby in a perambulator; its nanny informs the Auctioneers of its desire to return to its preferred, unborn state, of its immense personal fortune, and of her legally certified powers of proxy voting. In the event of its unbirthing she will be its sole heir.

Men and women of dubious background are present – outlaws, untouchables, outcasts. The security forces deal brusquely with many of these.

'Home' has become a scattered, damaged, hydra-various concept in our present travails. There is so much to yearn for. There are so few rainbows any more. How hard can we expect even a pair of magic shoes to work? Are metaphors comprehensible to them, abstractions permissible, redefinitions acceptable? Are we asking too much? As our needs emerge from their redoubts and press in upon the electrified glass, will the shoes, like the Grimms' ancient flatfish, lose patience with our demands and return us to the pisspots whence we came?

The presence of imaginary beings in the Saleroom may be the last straw. Children from nineteenth-century Australian realist paintings are here, whining from their ornate, gilded frames about being lost in the immensity of the outback. In blue smocks and ankle-socks they gaze into rain-forests and deserts. A literary character, condemned to an eternity of reading the works of Dickens to an armed madman in a jungle, has sent in a written bid. I notice, on a television monitor, the frail figure of an alien creature with an illuminated fingertip. This permeation of the real world by the fictional is a symptom of the moral decay of the culture of the millennium. Heroes step down off cinema screens and marry members of the audience. Will there be no end to it? Is the state employing insufficient violence? Should there be more rigorous controls? We debate such questions often. There can be little doubt that a large majority of us opposes the free, unrestricted migration of imaginary beings into an already damaged reality. Few of us, after all, would choose to travel in the opposite direction (though there are reports of an increase in such migrations latterly). I shelve such debates for the moment. The Auction is about to begin.

....

It is necessary that I speak about my cousin Gail, and her habit of moaning loudly while making love. My cousin Gail – let me be frank – is the love of my life, and even now that we have parted I can't forget the pleasure I derived from her noisiness. I hasten to add that except for this volubility there was nothing abnormal about our lovemaking, nothing, if I may put it thus, *fictional*. Yet it satisfied me deeply, especially when she cried out at the moment of penetration, 'Home, boy! Home, baby – you've come home!' One day, however, I came home to find her in the arms of a hairy escapee from a caveman movie. I moved out the same day, weeping my way down the street with my large portrait of Gail in the guise of a tornado cradled in my arms and my collection of old Pat Boone 78 rpm records in a rucksack on my back. This happened many years ago. For a time after Gail dumped me I was bitter and would reveal to our social circle that she had lost her virginity at the age of fourteen in an accident involving a defective shooting-stick, but vindictiveness did not satisfy me for long. Since those days I have dedicated myself to her memory. I have made of myself a candle at her temple. I am aware that after all these years the Gail I adore is not entirely a real person. The real Gail has become confused with my re-imagining of her, of our life together in an alternative universe devoid of ape-men. The real Gail may by now be beyond our grasp, ineffable.

I saw her recently, in a long dark subterranean bar guarded by commandos bearing battlefield nuclear weapons. There were Polynesian snacks on the counter and beers from the Pacific basin on tap: Kirin, Tsingtao, Swan. At that time many television channels were devoted to the sad case of the astronaut stranded on Mars without hope of rescue, and with diminishing supplies of food and breathable air. The cameras inside his marooned spacecraft continued to send us poignant images of his slow descent into despair, his low-gravity, weight-reduced death. I watched my cousin Gail watching the screen, and when this condemned man on another planet began to sing a squawky medley of songs I was reminded of the dying computer in *2001: A Space Odyssey*, which sang 'Daisy, Daisy' as it was being unplugged; but my cousin Gail, hearing these spaced-out renditions of 'Swanee', 'Show me the way to go home' and several numbers from *The Wizard of Oz*, began to weep. I first heard about the upcoming auction of the ruby slippers the very next morning, and resolved at once to buy them, whatever the cost. My plan was simple. I would offer them up to Gail in all humility. Perhaps I would even click the heels together three times; and I would win back her heart by murmuring softly: *There's no place like home.*

. . . .

You laugh at my desperation. Hah! Go tell a drowning man not to grab for the passing straws. Or a dying astronaut not to sing. Come here and stand in my shoes. Step across this line. Put 'em up. Put 'em uuup. I'll fight you with one hand tied behind my back. I'll fight you with my eyes closed. Scared, huh? Scared?

....

The Grand Saleroom of the Auctioneers is the beating heart of the world. If you stand here for long enough all the wonders of the world will pass by. In the Grand Saleroom, in recent years, we have witnessed the auction of the Taj Mahal, the Statue of Liberty, the Sphinx. We have assisted at the sale of wives and the purchase of husbands. State secrets have been sold here, openly, to the highest bidder. On one very special occasion, the Auctioneers presided over the sale, to an overheated bunch of smouldering red demons, of a wide selection of human souls of all classes, qualities, ages, races and creeds. Everything is for sale, and under the firm yet essentially benevolent supervision of the Auctioneers, their security dogs and SWAT teams, we engage in a battle of wits and wallets, a war of nerves. There is a purity about our actions here, and also an aesthetically pleasing tension between the vast complexity of the life that turns up, packaged into lots, to go under the hammer, and the equally immense simplicity of our manner of dealing with it. We bid, the Auctioneers knock a lot down, we pass on. All are equal before the justice of the gavels: the pavement artist and Michelangelo, the slave girl and the queen. This is the courtroom of demand.

They are bidding for the slippers now. As the price rises, so does my gorge. Panic is clutching at me, pulling me down, drowning me. I think of Gail – sweet coz! – and fight back the fear, and bid.

....

Once I was asked by the widower of a world-famous and much-loved pop singer to attend an auction of rock memorabilia on his behalf. He was the sole trustee of her estate, which was worth tens of millions; I treated him with respect. 'There's only one lot I want,' he said. 'Buy it at any price.' It was an article of clothing, a pair of edible rice-paper panties in peppermint flavour, purchased long ago in a store on (I think this was the name) Rodeo Drive. My employer's late wife's stage act had included the public removal and consumption of several such pairs. More panties, in a variety of flavours – chocolate chip, knickerbocker glory, cassata – were hurled into the crowd. These, too, were gobbled up in the excitement, the lucky recipients being too carried away to consider the future value of what they had caught. Undergarments that had actually been owned by the lady were therefore in short supply, and presently in great demand. During that auction, bids came in across the video links with Tokyo, Los Angeles, Paris and Milan, and they were so rapid and of such size that I lost my nerve. However, when I telephoned my employer to confess my failure he was quite unperturbed, interested only in the price the lot had fetched. I mentioned a five-figure sum, and he laughed. It was the first truly joyful laugh I had heard from him since the day his wife died. 'That's all right then,' he said. 'I've got three hundred thousand of those.'

It is to the Auctioneers we go to establish the value of our pasts, of our futures, of our lives.

The price for the ruby slippers is rising ever higher. Many of the bidders would appear to be proxies, as I was on the day of the underpants, as I am so often, in so many ways. Today, however, I am bidding – perhaps literally – for myself.

There's an explosion in the street outside. We hear running feet, sirens, screams. Such things have become commonplace. We remain absorbed by a higher drama.

The cuspidors are in full employment. Witches keen, movie stars flounce off with tarnished auras. Queues of the disconsolate form at the psychiatrists' booths. There is work for the club-wielding guards, though not, as yet, for the obstetricians. Order is maintained. I am the only person in the Grand Saleroom still in the bidding. My rivals are disembodied heads on video screens, and unheard voices on special telephone links. I am doing battle with an invisible world of demons and ghosts, and the prize is my lady's hand.

At the height of an auction, when the money has become no more than a way of keeping score, there is a thing that happens which I am reluctant to admit: one becomes detached from the earth. There is a loss of gravity, a reduction in weight, a floating in the capsule of the struggle. The ultimate goal crosses a delirious frontier. Its achievement and our own survival become – yes! – fictions.

And fictions, as I have come close to suggesting before, are dangerous.

In fiction's grip, we may mortgage our homes, sell our children, to have whatever it is we crave. Alternatively, in that miasmal ocean, we may simply float away from our hearts' desires, and see them anew, from a distance, so that they seem weightless, trivial. We let them go. Like men dying in a blizzard, we lie down in the snow to sleep.

So it is that my cousin Gail loses her hold over me in the crucible of the auction. So it is that I drop out of the bidding, and sleep.

When I awake I feel refreshed, and free.

Next week there is another auction. Family trees, coats of arms, royal lineages will be up for sale, and into any of these one may insert any name one chooses, one's own, or one's beloved's. Canine pedigrees will be on offer, too: Alsatian, saluki, Cairn terrier.

. . . .

Did I mention my love for my cousin Toto?

CREDITS

· ·

The Wizard of Oz

USA
1939
Production company
Loew's Incorporated
A Victor Fleming
Production
US release
25 August 1939
Distributor (US)
MGM
UK release
25 March 1940
Distributor (UK)
MGM
Copyright date
7 August 1939
Producer
Mervyn LeRoy
Associate producer
Arthur Freed
Director
Victor Fleming
Screenplay
Noel Langley, Florence
Ryerson, Edgar Allan
Woolf, from the book by
L. Frank Baum
Adaptation
Noel Langley
**Photography (sepia and
Technicolor)**
Harold Rosson
Associate photographer
Allen Davey
Music
Harold Arlen
Lyrics
E.Y. Harburg
Musical adaptation
Herbert Stothart
Associate conductor
George Stoll
**Orchestration and vocal
arrangements**
George Bassman, Murray
Cutter, Paul Marquardt,
Ken Darby

**Musical numbers staged
by**
Bobby Connolly
**Additional incidental
music**
George Bassman, George
Stoll, Robert Stringer
**Additional music
adaptation and additional
orchestration**
Roger Edens

Songs: 'Over the rainbow',
'Munchkinland', 'Ding dong,
the witch is dead', 'Follow
the yellow brick road',
'We're off to see the
Wizard', 'If I only had a
brain/a heart/the nerve', 'If I
were king of the forest',
'The merry old land of Oz',
by Arlen, Harburg;
'Munchkinland nos. 1–4' by
Arlen, Harburg, Edens;
'Threatening witch', 'Into
the forest of the wild beast',
'The city gates are open',
'At the gates of the Emerald
City', 'Magic smoke chords',
'Toto's chase', 'On the
castle wall', 'Delirious
escape', by Stothart; 'The
cornfields' by Stothart, Stoll,
Bassman; 'Poppies' by
Stothart, Stringer;
'Optimistic voices' by Arlen,
Stothart, Harburg; 'The
Witch's castle' by Stothart,
Mendelssohn; 'March of the
Winkies' by Stothart, Edens;
'Dorothy's rescue' (based on
Mussorgsky's 'Night on the
bald mountain') arranged by
Edens; 'In the shade of the
old apple tree' by Van
Alstyne

Editor
Blanche Sewell
Art director
Cedric Gibbons
Associate art director
William A. Horning
Set decorator
Edwin B. Willis
Assistant art directors
Jack Martin Smith,
Randall Duell
Backdrops
George Gibson
Sculptures
Henry Greutert
Costumes
Adrian
Wardrobe assistants
Vera Mordaunt, Marian
Parker, John B. Scura
Character make-up
Jack Dawn
Special effects
Arnold Gillespie
Special effects assistants
Franklin Milton,
Jack McMaster
Colour director
Natalie Kalmus
Associate colour director
Henri Jaffa
Technicolor assistants
Fred Detmers, Henry Imus
Recording director
Douglas Shearer
Animal trainer
Carl Spitz
101 minutes
9180 feet

Judy Garland
Dorothy Gale
Frank Morgan
Professor Marvel/The Wizard
Ray Bolger
Hunk/The Scarecrow
Bert Lahr
Zeke/The Cowardly Lion
Jack Haley
Hickory/The Tin Woodsman
Billie Burke
Glinda, The Good Witch
Margaret Hamilton
Miss Gulch/The Wicked Witch
Charley Grapewin
Uncle Henry
Pat Walshe
Nikko
Clara Blandick
Auntie Em
Terry
Toto the dog
The Singer Midgets
The Munchkins
Mitchell Lewis
Monkey Officer

and as Munchkins
performers: Gladys M.
Allison, John Ballas, Franz
Balluck, Josefine Balluck,
John T. Bambury, Charles
Becker, Freda Besky,
Yvonne Moray Bistany,
Henry Boers, Theodore
Boers, Christie Buresh,
Eduard Buresh, Lida
Buresh, Mickey Carroll,
Colonel Caspar, Nona
Cooper, Thomas J.
Cottonaro, Elizabeth
Coulter, Frank H. Cucksey,
Billy Curtis, Eugene S.
David Jr, Eulie H. David,
Ethel W. Denis, Prince
Denis, Hazel I. Derthick,
Major Doyle, Carl M.
Erickson, Jannette Fern,
Addie E. Frank, Thaisa L.
Gardner, Jakob Gerlich,
Bill Giblin, Jack Glicken,
Carolyn E. Granger, Joseph
Herbst, Jakob Hofbauer,
Major Mite (= C.C.
Howerton), Helen M. Hoy,
Marguerite A. Hoy, James
R. Hulse, Lord Roberts (=
Kanter), Charles Kelley,
Jessie E. Kelley, Frank
Kikel, Bernhard Klima,
Emma Koestner, Mitzi
Koestner, Willi Koestner,
Carl Kosiczky, Adam Edwin
Kozieki, Joseph J. Koziel,
Dolly Kramer, Emil
Kranzler, Nita Krebs, Jeane
LaBarbera, Hilda Lange,
John Leal, Ann Rice Leslie,
Idaho Lewis (= L.A. Croft),
Charles Ludwig, Carlos
Manzo, Howard Marco,
Jerry Maren (= Gerard
Marenghi), Bela Matina,
Lajos Matina, Matthew

Matina, Walter M.B. Miller,
George Minister, Harry
Monty, Olga C. Nardone,
Nels Nelson, Margaret C.H.
Nickloy, Franklin H.
O'Baugh, William H.
O'Docharty, Hildred C.
Olson, Frank Packard,
Nicholas Page, Leona Parks,
Margaret Pellegrini, Johnny
Pizo, Prince Leon (=
Polinsky), Lillian Porter,
Meinhardt Raabe, Margaret
Raia, Matthew Raia, Hazel
Resmondo, Little Billy (=
Rhodes), Gertrude H. Rice,
Hazel Rice, Friedrich Ritter,
Ruth L. Robinson, Sandor
Roka, Jimmie Rosen,
Charles F. Royale, Helen J.
Royale, Albert Ruddinger,
Elly A. Schneider, Frieda
Schneider, Hilda E.
Schneider, Kurt Schneider,
Elsie R. Schultz, Charles
Silvern, Garland Slatten,
Ruth E. Smith, Elmer
Spangler, Pernell E. St.
Aubin, Carl Stephan, Alta
M. Stevens, George Suchsie,
Charlotte V. Sullivan,
Clarence Swensen, Betty
Tanner (= Titus), Arnold
Vierling, Gus Wayne, Victor
Wetter, Grace G. Williams,
Harvey B. Williams,
Margaret Williams, John
Winters (= Maroldo),
Gladys V. Wolff, Murray
Wood

Note: The following directors worked on *The Wizard of Oz* but were uncredited: Richard Thorpe (two weeks), George Cukor (three days), King Vidor (ten days). The following writers were also hired, but were uncredited: Herman J. Mankiewicz, Ogden Nash (no contribution used), Herbert Fields (no contribution used), Samuel Hoffenstein, Jack Mintz, Sid Silvers (no contribution used), John Lee Mahin.

Other films based on the books of L. Frank Baum include:
The Wizard of Oz
(dir. Otis Turner, 1910)
The Patchwork Girl of Oz
(dir. J. Farrell MacDonald, 1914)
The Magic Cloak of Oz
(dir. L. Frank Baum, 1914)
The Wizard of Oz
(dir. Larry Semon, 1925)
Journey Back to Oz
(dir. Hal Sutherland, 1971)
The Wiz
(dir. Sidney Lumet, 1978)
Dorothy in the Land of Oz
(dir. Charles Swenson, 1980, for TV)
Under the Rainbow
(dir. Steve Rash, 1981)
The Wizard of Oz
(Japanese animated film, 1982)
Return to Oz
(dir. Walter Murch, 1985)
The Wonderful Wizard of Oz
(Australian animated film, 1989)
That's Dancing
(dir. Jack Haley Jr, 1985) includes a Ray Bolger scene cut from the release print of *The Wizard of Oz*. The laser disc 'Collector's Edition' of the film includes further material cut from the film as released.

The print of *The Wizard of Oz* in the National Film Archive was specially acquired from Turner Entertainment, who hold distribution rights.

BIBLIOGRAPHY

· ·

Cox, Stephen. *The Munchkins Remember: The Wizard of Oz and Beyond* (New York: E.P. Dutton, 1989)

Fordin, Hugh. *The World of Entertainment: Hollywood's Greatest Musicals* (Garden City, New York: Doubleday, 1975)

Fricke, John; Scarfone, Jay; Stillman, William. *The Wizard of Oz: the Official 50th Anniversary Pictorial History* (New York: Warner Brooks, 1989)

Harmetz, Aljean. *The Making of the Wizard of Oz* (New York: Doubleday/Dell Books, 1989)

Hearn, Michael Patrick (ed.). *The Wizard of Oz: The Screenplay* (New York: Bantam Doubleday/Dell Books, 1989)

Jablonski, Edward. *Harold Arlen: Happy with the Blues* 2nd ed. (New York: Da Capo, 1986)

Lahr, John. *Notes on a Cowardly Lion* (New York, Alfred A. Knopf, 1969)

LeRoy, Mervyn. *Mervyn LeRoy: Take One* (New York, Hawthorn, 1974)

McClelland, Doug. *Down the Yellow Brick Road: The Making of the Wizard of Oz* (New York: Bonanza Books, 1989)

Schatz, Thomas. *The Genius of the System: Hollywood Film Making in the Studio Era* (New York: Pantheon, 1988)

BFI FILM

CLASSICS

Each book in the BFI Film Classics series honours a great film from the history of world cinema. With four new titles published each spring and autumn, the series will rapidly build into a collection representing some of the best writing on film. Forthcoming titles include *Citizen Kane* by Laura Mulvey, *The Big Heat* by Colin McArthur, *Brief Encounter* by Richard Dyer and *L'Atalante* by Marina Warner.

If you would like to receive further information about future BFI Film Classics or about other books on film, media and popular culture from BFI Publishing, please fill in your name and address below and return the card to the BFI.

No stamp is needed if posted in the United Kingdom, Channel Islands, or Isle of Man.

NAME

ADDRESS

POSTCODE

BFI Publishing
21 Stephen Street
FREEPOST 7
LONDON
W1E 4AN